BRITAIN IN OLD F   HS

BARNSLEY
1890s–1990s

BRIAN ELLIOTT

SUTTON PUBLISHING LIMITED

Sutton Publishing Limited
Phoenix Mill · Thrupp · Stroud
Gloucestershire · GL5 2BU

First published 1999

British Library Cataloguing in Publication Data
A catalogue record for this book is available from the
British Library.

ISBN 0-7509-2269-9

Typeset in 10.5/13.5 Photina.
Typesetting and origination by
Sutton Publishing Limited.
Printed in Great Britain by
Ebenezer Baylis, Worcester.

Title page photograph: A mobile trader allows his horse to drink from the trough at Eldon/Kendray Street, one of a superb series of Barnsley photographs produced by Warner Gothard and published in the mid-1890s as *Views of Barnsley & Neighbourhood.* Across Eldon Street tailor Scholey and Popplewell's 'Shaving and Hair-Cutting' saloon are open for business. The dominating building is the Harvey Institute, so named in honour of local JP Charles Harvey who 'gifted' the building to the town twelve years after it had been built by a private company in 1876–77 at a cost of £27,000, functioning as the Public and Mechanics' Hall.

Market Hill, *c.* 1890. The interesting façades of buildings overlook the broad space where stalls were erected on market days at the heart of the medieval town. The five-bay building near the bottom of the hill is the King's Head Hotel, believed to be where the Barnsley Chop was 'invented' to cater for the hunger of visiting farmers and tradesmen. The late Georgian coaching inn was built on the site of the home of the Wood family, prominent solicitors and magistrates.

CONTENTS

Aerial view of the town, 1989. Much of its medieval layout is still apparent despite massive changes to the built environment during the twentieth century.

INTRODUCTION

Even within the context of the industrial towns of the north of England Barnsley has undergone massive changes to both its built environment and economic base over the last hundred years. The old textile mills from which the town had earned such a high reputation during the previous century had long been exhausted by the Edwardian period, though many buildings remained. Glassmaking continues to be an important local industry but great family concerns such as Rylands and Woods have gone. In the early 1970s an eighty-year-old member of the writer's local history class was able to plot more than sixty collieries on a commercial street plan of Barnsley: some large with familiar names such as Barnsley Main and Wharncliffe Woodmoor; others, like Primrose, Slack and Penny Pie, small and less well known – but all sunk during the late nineteenth and early twentieth century when coal was king. After 1945 there continued to be a huge demand for coal, but though nationalisation was welcomed the first large pit closures of the 1960s were modest compared with the wholesale, many would say vengeful, closure of all Barnsley area mines in the years following the 1984–85 strike.

Today there are few obvious pre-Victorian buildings in the old urban heart of the town and yet – despite the legacy of '60s and '70s 'redevelopment' – it is still possible to trace the medieval layout, especially from the air. Modern research methods continue to help us understand how Barnsley evolved over time, but there will be much to do and much to interpret during the 'information age', and still a great need to record the changing scene. On the ground evidence continues to reveal clues to its past, for example, on Butterfield's site, which was redeveloped in 1999.

This book is not intended as a miscellaneous collection of old photographs, though many examples will, understandably, evoke nostalgic interest. Rather it is an attempt to show people and places alongside continuity as well as change. To this end there has been a careful choice of themes, including sport and recreation as well as the world of work: hard times and happy times. Inevitably there are limitations and omissions within such a wide time-span.

Barnsley was blessed with some excellent Edwardian photographers. We owe much to the pioneering exploits of the likes of professionals such as Gothard, Lamb, Irving and Randall, and enterprising publishers such as Haigh at a time when a picture postcard sent in the morning arrived at a local destination a few hours later: not as instant as today's e-mail but a very efficient and pleasant way of communication.

For the later period it was particularly refreshing for the writer to be able to include some of the unpublished work from the camera of miner and pit deputy Irvin Harris, and to gain the support and confidence of several individuals and families who were kind enough to loan photographs. The theme of the book would have been the worse but for their co-operation. The bulk of the illustrations are from the author's own collection and camera, but many thanks are also due to the unselfish help of Chris and Pearl Sharpe of *Old Barnsley* and to Kath Parkin and her excellent 'Memories' feature in the *Barnsley Chronicle* whose readers, despite the passage of time, have provided some amazing identifications of people and subjects. The author would also particularly like to extend his appreciation to Lord Mason of Barnsley for his kindness at allowing access to his vast collection of photographs; to the Tasker Photographic Trust; and to Simon Fletcher of Sutton for his encouragement of the project.

Since the 1984–85 miners' strike there has been an explosion of poems, prose and well-researched historical writing from Barnsley people. As we enter the new millennium, despite all the hype, there is much to celebrate about Barnsley's past while its continued regeneration through the work of individuals, businesses and partnerships have and are already transforming the town and district.

Some of the best and most contrasting landscapes and scenery in the north of England lie within the present Barnsley Metropolitan Council area, but thankfully, despite all the changes and urban conformity, its people continue to give the place a life and character all of its own.

Pitt Street was one of the most elegant parts of town, as can be seen in this Edwardian postcard. The Wesleyan chapel and smaller 'Temperance Hall' are clearly visible but 'x' marks the entrance to Dr Blackburn's house. Interestingly, this card only took nine days to reach the 'Hudson Terminal' in north-east USA in 1909. Two years earlier the *Lusitania* had sailed across the Atlantic in under four days.

CHAPTER ONE

MARKET HILL & CHURCH STREET

The bottom of Market Hill has activity even on a non-market day on this postcard franked in 1903; but the photographic original must have been taken on or before 1900 since John Aspinall's millinery shop, then at the corner of Eldon Street, is still standing. Note the policeman and boys no doubt interested in the photographer's actions.

This fine Gothard view of *c.* 1895 shows Aspinall's business 'established 1863' (though from here in 1873) in more detail. Hats were of course in great demand and fill his shop window. A fairly quiet time of day, but it helps us see the 'cobbled' (stone-setted) street surfaces. The distinctive Coach and Horses Hotel at the bottom of the hill – at the junction with Peel Street – was built in 1857 and remained an inn until 1911. At the top of the hill, by Shambles Street, we can just glimpse the Corn Exchange which was burnt down in 1927.

A procession of some importance involving horse-drawn vehicles proceeds down Market Hill. The relief of Ladysmith in the South African (Boer) War took place at the end of February 1900, but this may relate to a more local event, and may be a year or two later.

This superb view of the bottom of Market Hill is so clear that parts of posters can be read at the corner of the Coach and Horses. The new and ornate Yorkshire Penny Bank building with its clock (at noon) and 1903 datestone (but with offices still 'To Let') makes the late Edwardian scene more familiar to the modern eye. *Tasker Photographic Trust*

Market stalls are in place in this view of about 1910, serviced no doubt by horse-drawn vehicles of the type shown in the picture.

'The Hill' came to life at the annual Monday afternoon Whit gathering, organised by the Sunday School Union, on this occasion in 1907. It was the highlight of the summer for local children when the streets were lined with onlookers, many of them proud parents. Various churches and chapels proudly display their banners and, assisted by a printed programme, members sang hymns, usually to the accompaniment of a military band.

Some of Barnsley's first cars begin to appear on picture postcards during the first decade of the century, when it was legal to drive at up to 20 mph, but at busy times town centre traffic must have been more chaotic than shown here – noisy cars mixing with horse-drawn vehicles, and no lane discipline on streets littered with manure.

Another crowded Whit Monday scene on Market Hill, 1910, a veritable sea of hats and caps (and one or two police helmets) skilfully captured by T. Lamb of Racecommon Road, one of Barnsley's best picture postcard photographers. A collection would have been taken on the hill and along the route of the procession.

The Royals (King George V and Queen Mary) welcomed – note the carpet and line of waiting dignitaries – at the bottom of Market Hill, 12 July 1912. The building just visible in the background is the former Coach & Horses which had just been converted into the London City and Midland Bank. In the foreground several professional photographers can be seen with tripods and bulky large-frame camera equipment.

Seven years after the end of the First World War the official 'unveiling' of the war memorial understandably attracted large crowds to Church Street, Sunday 11 October 1925. Several thousand young men had been quick to respond to Kitchener's call to arms when the country was so ill-prepared for war, but the volunteers known as the Barnsley Pals (13th and 14th Battalions of the York and Lancaster Regiment) sustained horrible losses, particularly on the Somme in 1916.

Laying the foundation stone for Barnsley's new town hall, Thursday 21 April 1932. The ceremony was performed by Mayor Jonas Plummer JP, who said that when opened the 'noble and inspiring building' would also inspire present and future councillors when deliberating upon borough affairs.

The emerging town hall tower covered with scaffolding during the winter of 1932–33, its neo-classical design already apparent. It had been estimated that a hundred men would be employed during each week of construction 'assisting the government in the relief of the unemployment of the Borough'.

The 'New Town Hall' shown on this 1930s postcard officially opened on Thursday 14 December 1933, HRH the Prince of Wales ceremonially unlocking the door with a golden key. George Orwell (Eric Blair) was highly critical of the expense of the building in his book *The Road to Wigan Pier* (1937), following a two-week stay in the town in March 1936 when he visited working class houses; but alongside the new Mining and Technical College the transformation of the west of Church Street, which had begun with slum clearances a decade earlier, was now complete – and Barnsley had one of the most distinctive public buildings in the north of England.

Market Hill and Church Street on a quiet Sunday afternoon in September 1981, the old market area having recently been planted with a few trees but also ignominiously set aside for the parking of a few cars.

The National Westminster Bank (NatWest) with its classical façade remains one of Barnsley's finest buildings. It is seen here on the same day as the picture above. Built on the site of the old King's Head, it was occupied by the Sheffield Banking Company Limited from 1915, but many Barnsley people will remember it as the National Provincial.

GEORGE GUEST,

MARKET HILL,

BARNSLEY,

AGENT FOR

HUNTLEY AND PALMER'S
READING BISCUITS.

Crosse and Blackwell's

PICKLES, SAUCES & CONDIMENTS

FRY & SONS' COCOAS & CHOCOLATES.

EPPS' Homœopathic COCOA

Cantrell and Cochrane's

Ginger Ale, Aerated Waters, Lemonade, &c.

MILNER'S FIRE AND THIEF-PROOF SAFES.

EAGLE LIFE INSURANCE COMPY.

SUN FIRE OFFICE.

RAILWAY   PASSENGERS'   ACCIDENT   ASSURANCE   COMPANY.

An advertisement for George Guest, 1914. The shop's stock of fine teas, coffees, cheeses, bacon and hams created an unmistakable aroma that had attracted several generations of discerning customers even before the making of the Arcade in 1893. Later the upstairs restaurant became a popular facility.

The old Guest's building now (April 1999) functions as a Durty O'Dwyers, an example of the many (some would say too many) theme pubs that proliferate the town.

Henry Elstone's originally opened in 1857 on Market Hill, with a rear warehouse in George's Yard, as a wholesale tobacco importer. As a tobacconist's shop over four generations it diversified into fine teas and coffees, jams, Christmas puddings and so on, even newspapers and magazines. Here in this 1938 photograph we can see Mr Brown (left) who managed the shop for fifty years, Miss Ada Humpleby (assistant) and, in charge of the wholesale department, Harold Farnsworth.

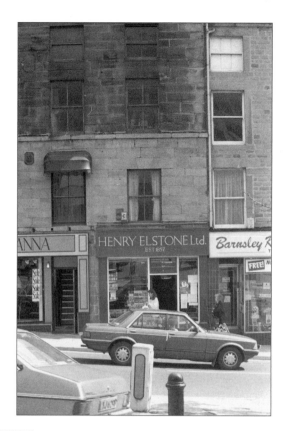

Elstone's in its twilight years, summer 1988. It sold newspapers and magazines at this time and even stocked the author's first published local histories of Royston parish.

Continuity and change is apparent in this modern photograph. The former Elstone shop, now (April 1999) Danjo's boutique, is next to Pizza Americano, the former premises of a succession of chemists such as Rock (mid-1950s–'70s), Wilson (1930s–mid-'50s) and Moorhouse (from 1903).

The Georgian White Bear Inn on Church Street, seen here in 1981, changed its name to the Royal Hotel following the visit of the Duchess of Kent and Princess Victoria in 1835, landlady Hawksworth supplying fresh post-horses for the royal carriage. In 1988 Sheffield brewers Wards abused planning regulations by adding canopies and a two-tone colour scheme to the Grade II listed building. The closure of Thom's Store (owned by Poundstretcher), formerly part of Butterfield & Massie's popular department store, and its subsequent deterioration while empty over almost ten years, created a massive eyesore on a prime and historic site for most of the 1990s.

The Thom's property was sold in February 1998, and work was quickly instigated to re-develop the site. The frontage of part of the Butterfield's complex (that adjoined the Royal, now Fealty & Firkin) with its blocked Palladian window was dismantled, but rebuilt in a sympathetic style. Interestingly, contractors discovered the remains of timber framing that has been dated by dendrochronology to late medieval times, confirming the long occupational continuity of the site since rich mercers (dealers in fine fabrics) were resident in this area from at least the seventeenth century.

Advertising postcard of Alfred James, watchmaker and jeweller, who traded from 1894 to 1907 from a shop that occupied the lower two bays of the ground floor of the Royal Hotel. For a short time (1908–10) the shop was leased to jeweller Benjamin Harral after the closure of his first shop at the Market Hill end of Eldon Street; but Harral was already developing his gleaming new Ring Shop further along Eldon Street.

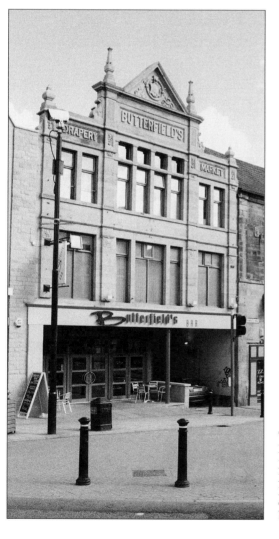

The distinctive and attractive façade of Butterfield's Drapery Market was retained and carefully restored, 'Butterfield's' pub/restaurant opening its doors in December 1998. This photograph was taken in April 1999. The next major project, already given planning permission, will be the development of George Yard, in particular the Beehive building and nearby linen warehouse.

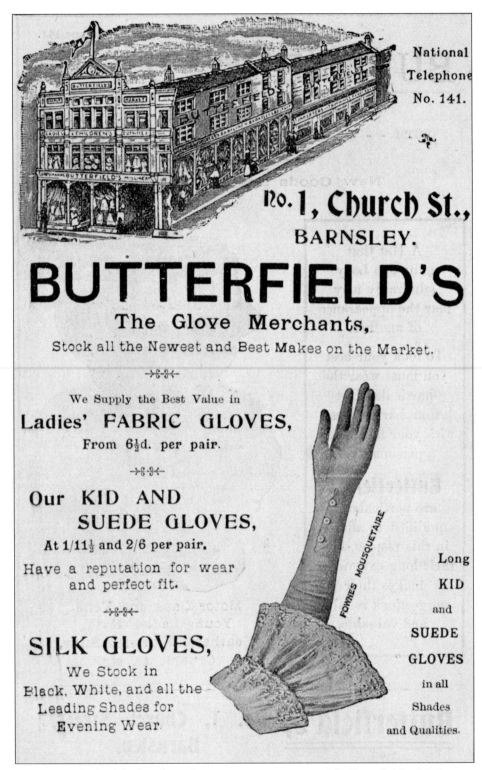

One of a series of splendid Edwardian advertisements commissioned by Butterfield's, 1908.

TOWN STREETS & SHOPS

A Barnsley Electric Company tram is driven via Eldon Street and from Kendray Street towards May Day Green on what appears to be market day, c. 1910. Services commenced in November 1902 with ten cars. At about 1d a mile they were seen as the people's transport, soon carrying more than two million passengers a year. The last commercially run tram travelled on this system in August 1930.

An early view of Peel Square with horse-drawn cabs waiting for custom, from the camera of Warner Gothard, 1895. The Barnsley Coffee Tavern Company had occupied a suite of upper rooms in the dominating block (despite the sign better known as the Chronicle Buildings) overlooking the square since 1879 (in the Temperance era), but ceased trading in 1903, the year that motorised taxis first appeared in London.

A contrasting view of Peel Square in 1992, when pedestrianisation was in progress. The old Chronicle Buildings had been used principally for banking purposes since the demolition of the nearby Imperial Hotel in the late 1950s, functioning as the TSB at the time of the photograph. In 1994 Tetley's Brewery took over, naming the converted pub Tommy Wallocks after two famous local characters, following a *Barnsley Chronicle* competition.

Above: The Fun Fair came to town with traditional and futuristic attractions, providing an unusual but more recent view of Peel Square. The photograph was taken from the vantage point of the mysterious pink granite-faced circular podium which was placed there at a cost of £20,000 (via the Government's Urban Programme Scheme) – perhaps to liven up the paving – in 1993. Some local comments about it are unprintable.

Right: Ironmongers M. Lowrance and Sons traded from several premises in the town centre, servicing collieries and builders and making 'The Barnsley' for discerning customers, as in this Edwardian advertisement.

When viewed from the top of what used to be called Pinfold Hill (Sackville Street) in 1910, the Townend area of Barnsley, with its small park in the foreground (opened with great pomp and ceremony on 29 June 1905) and old mill chimneys, assumes a Lowry-like appearance. Notice the flag flying from the Olympia Skating Rink, erected in 1909 but converted to the Pavilion Cinema in about 1920. It was destroyed by fire thirty years later.

George F. Banks (1893–1964) outside his Barnsley tobacconist's shop, probably mid-1930s. Such photographs are quite rare but of considerable interest to local and family historians.

Such is the pace of modern urban redevelopment that once familiar views disappear almost overnight and are soon forgotten. They are always worth recording for future generations. This photograph was taken by the author in 1981 from St George's Church, looking northwards along Yorks Street to Townend and Summer Lane.

This view, from the same vantage point as the photograph above, was taken in April 1999. A new roundabout had replaced the old six-laned junction in the summer of 1991 as part of the construction of the c. £7 million Western Relief Road. Many familiar buildings such as the former York Street Labour Exchange and, at the bottom of Racecommon Road, the Wheatsheaf Hotel and Town End Stores were demolished.

Another modern but historically significant view, taken in 1992 shortly after the completion of the Townend roundabout. In the distance is old St George's Church, Pitt Street, redundant since 1981 but one of the town's most important landmark buildings. St George's was a 'Waterloo Church', one of several built with funds generated by a grateful government to commemorate the famous victory of 1815. It was erected in 1821 (though later enlarged several times) to the design of Thomas Rickman, famous for his lectures on architectural styles. He employed iron in its construction, the deterioration of which contributed to its abandonment and sad loss.

The same view, spring 1999. Old St George's was demolished during late September/early October 1993 and the congregation now worships in the new church on York Street, built in 1980.

St George's Church as it appeared on an Edwardian picture postcard, *c.* 1903.

Interior of St George's, 1986, one of a series
of photographs taken by the author at a time
when severe vandalism was hastening its
decline. Many interior features had already
been sold but the stained glass windows were
often the targets of stone-throwing youths.

The central part of the 'Light of the World' window, based on a painting by the Pre-Raphaelite William Holman Hunt, symbolically showing Jesus with lantern in one hand and knocking at a door with the other, was rescued from the old church and placed in the new building in 1987, during the Rev. Jim Dainty's ministry.

Methodism made a significant impact in northern industrial towns such as Barnsley, though the Temperance movement was less successful. The Primitive Methodists established their place of worship in a commanding position on Westgate, used by the Barnsley Boys' Club from 1950 but, after several recent years of disuse, converted into the Lamproom Theatre in 1999. The large Pitt Street Wesleyan church of 1846 was photographed by the author just prior to its demolition in 1984. Next door the Temperance Hall, commissioned by the Oddfellows a decade earlier, became Thomas Dale's auction mart, then (1880–97) was used by Barnsley Temperance Society. Afterwards it successively served as a cinema, dancing school, warehouse, and after 1990s refurbishment and enlargement as another theme pub – but at least it survives, perhaps the only elegant building on what was once, architecturally, the best street in Barnsley.

This view of Cheapside and Queen Street dates from about 1910 and shows a number of well-known traders on prime sites near the expanding market area. On the right and of particular note is Benjamin Gaunt & Sons, who having expanded his corner premises in about 1890 continued to trade here until 1929, when this and neighbouring properties were demolished and largely replaced by F.W. Woolworth's new store which extended back to Eldon Street.

Quite a contrast: Cheapside and Queen Street on a summer Saturday in 1992. Woolworth's modern store, with its distinctive vertical panelling, had opened in 1974 but ceased trading in March 1984, its last sale a bunk-bed.

A busy day at the bottom of Market Hill with Queen Street properties in the background; but notice the narrow width of the street. Two bowler-hatted Edwardian gentlemen are in conversation by Reynolds & Wadsworth, the ironmonger's, an assortment of shovels, buckets, trunks and so on adding interest to the scene. *Tasker Photographic Trust*

A contrasting view, April 1999, with part of the Fun Fair sited along a much wider Queen Street and pedestrianised Cheapside. McDonald's is now well established in the 1930s Burton's building, Marks & Spencer is across the street and adjacent old properties have been demolished and rebuilt with some architectural sympathy to their predecessors, hence the mock-Palladian window.

Queen Street on a sunny day in the 1950s. Burton's the tailors, the Three Cranes Hotel, the Royal Oak and just part of F.W. Woolworth's store are in view on the left side of the photograph. There is not much traffic for shoppers to worry about.

A wonderful view of Cheapside, possibly in about 1912–13 when Hudson's had established their new Dining Rooms. With the flags, banners and decoration there appears to be a distinct air of patriotic and/or royal celebration. *Tasker Photographic Trust*

By 1919 the Barnsley and District Electric Traction Company – even though its tram services were doing well – had dropped the word Electric from its name in view of the fast-developing omnibus business. Here we can see one of its early buses passing along Cheapside. By 1925 the fleet had expanded to 118 vehicles, all Leylands; the maximum speed remained at 12 mph.

The magnificent façade of the former Alhambra Cinema in the 1960s when it was reduced to functioning as the Vale Bingo Club. Built in 1915 as a 2,600 seater theatre, it was converted to a cinema in 1926, attracting film-goers for thirty-four years. It was demolished in the late 1980s.

During the golden age of the cinema great queues assembled for double-feature programmes, though it's not possible to assess the popularity of this programme, advertised in 1939. The Ray Milland film was described as a comedy and the John Howard/Heather Angel programme as 'an adventure involving international spies'.

A Dearne District Light Railway tram on Doncaster Road, by the Alhambra. The company's main service, which began in 1924, was a 14-mile route to Thurnscoe via Wombwell, Wath and Bolton-upon-Dearne, with spurs to Manvers Main Crossing and Swinton. It was often troubled by subsidence and flooding. The last journey was in September 1933.

The name Alhambra was chosen for Barnsley's new shopping mall, designed by Greycoat Shopping Centres and said to be costing £25m when futuristic plans and drawings were published in the *Barnsley Chronicle* of 23 January 1987. Here we can see early work in progress during the summer of 1988, shoppers going about their business below a huge crane and electronic notice board.

Barnsley's answer to Meadowhall? A view of the domed Alhambra Centre taken on a busy Saturday afternoon in April 1999, contrasting with very uninspiring 1960s architecture (despite a series of expensive redevelopments) on the approach via Cheapside. At least the Fun Fair adds some interest. The CRS (Co-op) Living store kept the Centre alive in the early years, but at the time of writing (July 1999) have now moved out of what they originally described as their flagship enterprise.

The very different sides of New Street, photographed in 1997, shortly after the Alhambra Centre opened. Bailey's, the shop that supplied 'all but the Baby' – one of Barnsley's oldest family businesses – was soon to close, its famous stork sign being salvaged and taken to Elsecar Heritage Centre.

In the early 1900s New Street accommodated a variety of small businesses. At the top of the street (Island Corner) we can see part of the impressive premises of the Barnsley British Co-operative Society, and on the right the sign for Lodge, the printer. Note the extra-large spectacles displayed above R.E. Gray's optician's shop, which traded from this site from 1898 to 1927.

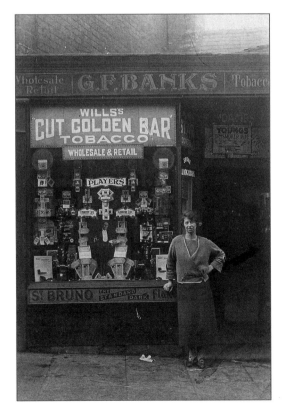

An interesting and rare photographic example of a small New Street shop: the premises of George F. Banks who traded both wholesale and retail.

Some indication of the grandeur of the Barnsley British Co-op Central premises is evident from this artist's impression, published in a commemorative history (celebrating the establishment of the first co-op town shop sixty years earlier) in 1902.

Another bird's-eye view of the Co-op headquarters taken from the direction of Market Street, the BBCS flag proudly flying from the main building, 1902.

The Co-op headquarters, Wellington Street, has a superb façade and is deservedly a listed building, though the lower part looks rather bedraggled with its 'for sale' notice at the centre in 1992.

It's remarkable how building usage changes in modern times. Transformation of the old Co-op building into a spectacular £2m nightclub was, after an initial refusal, given the go-ahead in June 1993. The red ribbon for the transformation was duly cut in December of the same year when it opened as Club Hedonism, but in April 1999 is shown as Hedon Rock, prelude to a proposed *c.* £1 million division into two clubs.

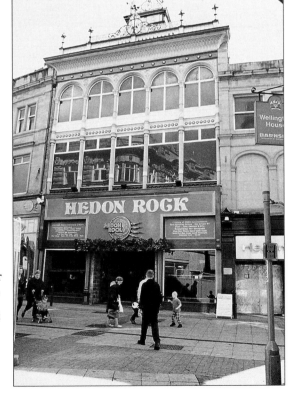

When we raise our eyes above street level in an urban setting it is surprising what architectural detail can be appreciated. The ornate façade of the upper part of the old Co-op building on Wellington Street, at the junction with Market Street, has very attractive features. This photograph dates from 1992.

Smartly dressed in their 'uniform' suits and smart dresses, staff at the BBCS offices, Wellington Street, c. 1933, photographed by A.J. Roberts of Barnsley. Back row, left to right: Tom Challenger, -?-, George Walker, Bill Sayles, Ernest Denton, Charles Barnham, Walter Norbron, Edward Armitage, Emmanuel Cherry. Third row: George Morray, Harold Robinson, Winifred Townsend, Busby John Briggs, Sidney Charles Richardson, Lucy Walker, Miss E. Rose, Winifred Gaunt, Connie Armitage, and Irene Oldham. Second row: Frank Squires, Frank Marshall, Oscar Palfreyman, Horace Pickering, Emmanuel Cherry, James Cook, Arthur Crick, William Turner and Cecil Whitham. Front row: James Hastie, Lawrence Crick, Percy Crowther, Leslie Barnham, Alfred Barber, Leslie Brown, Donald Overhead.

An early view of Eldon Street, taken from the bottom of Market Hill, before the extension to the Yorkshire Penny Bank which began in 1914.

Opposite, above: Eric Banks outside his Wellington Street confectionery and tobacco shop, shortly before its closure in 1984. Mr Banks had traded from this site, always popular with Theatre Royal customers, for more than fifty years.

Below: Shops often put on spectacular window displays during the Victorian and Edwardian era, and especially at Christmas, but here we see an example of early sponsorship, via Rowntree's most famous product, Mars bars, *c.* 1960.

Warner Gothard's photograph studio, sandwiched between Holdroyd the tailor's and Brown, the ironmonger's, on Eldon Street, *c.* 1900. Although a relatively distant view, such was the detail of large-frame cameras that some shop contents are clearly visible. The blurred image on the street is not a ghost but a person or horse moving too fast for the long exposure that would have been required. Notice the hoardings at the front of vacant building sites towards the end of the street.

Gothards produced thousands of *cartes de visite* and cabinet images, often of very high quality, that have survived in fine condition to the present day. Unfortunately few examples can be identified, especially when they turn up at antique and postcard fairs. Here is a typical anonymous example (of a man and wife?) in cabinet form from the Gothard studio, probably dating from about 1890, from the author's growing collection.

The spectacular upper façade of Benjamin Harral's Ring Shop, photographed by the author in 1982. Note the exterior clock, under which many people would arrange to meet. Part of the façade was lost on its conversion to an estate agent's in 1988.

A typical advertisement for the Ring Shop, dating from 1914. When purchasing an engagement or wedding ring customers were often presented with a commemorative gift – in my case a cake knife!

Eldon Street and the Harvey Institute on a Sunday in the early 1900s. The children that have gathered around the fountain and horse trough make this a most appealing picture. Denton's toy shop (est. 1852) next to Edwin Bayford's (no. 24), which sold 'Underclothing, Aprons, Corsets, Fancy Hosiery', and his 'Velveteen and Fent Warehouse' can be seen in the background. The two men in the foreground are also curious about the photographer's antics. *Tasker Photographic Trust*

Huge cheering crowds greeted William Booth (1829–1912) founder and general of the Salvation Army when he visited Barnsley on 11 August 1905; he is seen here arriving at the Harvey Institute. He was transported by a four-seater cab pulled by a grey horse, but his tour had been supported on Cheapside and Kendray Street by open-topped trams and an early motor vehicle. A replica canopy has recently (April 1999) been placed in position, but the Civic Theatre closed in 1998.

The original design of the
Barnsley Mechanics' Institute and
Public Hall, published in the
journal *The Builder*, 9 March
1878. The architect was a Mr Hill
of Leeds, and he produced a
ground-floor plan showing
provision for a library, reading
room, news room, lecture room
and two classrooms, with shops
incorporated within the west
wing. Above was the Official
School of Art and Public Hall; in
total it had accommodation for
1,700–1,800 people.

The Hall has had a chequered history, the saddest occasion being commemorated in the hurriedly produced
Gothard postcard sent from Worsbrough Bridge on 16 January (a Thursday) in 1908. On the Saturday, only five
days earlier, incoming children had been told to descend a twisting stone staircase and enter by the main entrance
where they would be admitted to the pit for the same price. Unfortunately many others were ascending at the
same time, and in the resultant chaos sixteen children, aged four to eight, were crushed to death.

This is an early view (possibly printed from a magic lantern slide) of Kendray Street, showing Robinson's saw mill and part of Barnsley's industrial skyline in the 1890s. The fountain and horse trough at the Eldon Street junction, funded by Mrs Ann Lambert, were erected in 1887 in honour of her parents, Francis and Ann Kendray. Notice the advertising hoardings seen in more detail below.

Twentieth-century marketing departments could have taught the Victorians little, as anyone who has trawled through local newspapers will confirm. Here we have a splendid array of fly posters of products and events at the corner of Kendray Street and Queen's Road.

Mallinson's of Eldon Street, *c.* 1907. The shop sold pit (mine) and many other kinds of ropes; it was a family concern that could trace its origins to the eighteenth century. Posters outside the bookseller's and newsagent's shop provide us with a fascinating reminder of the immense importance of the printed word. Papers were the source of news before the invention of the wireless, numerous independent street vendors selling the latest editions. The barber's pole is outside what was probably Alfred Joynes' shop.

Looking up lower Regent Street from the Yorkshire Traction bus station when the Court House (opposite the blackened Queen's Hotel) was used by L. Goodworth, wholesale draper; the Congregational church (built 1856) is the most striking feature. The old railway bridge, for so long a familiar landmark (and advertising space), had recently been demolished, while the church received the same fate in 1971. This photograph was taken by the author in 1968.

The Regent Street Court House station, a Grade II listed building, was refurbished by Wetherspoons and reopened in April 1999 at the time this photograph was taken; the previous name, Comedy Shop, was thankfully abandoned. Built as the town court house in 1861, it was transformed into the Court House railway station in 1870 until its closure ninety years later.

CHAPTER THREE

SCHOOL DAYS

School Street, Darfield, early 1900s. Children (and a dog) have assembled across the street and a horse-drawn milk cart is just in view. This is an apparently informal scene captured by the local photographer (W. Stables, whose studio was behind the Rising Sun Inn, Snape Hill), but there were obvious sales advantages in attracting people to enhance the scene. Notice the barber who peers out of his shop doorway. Old Barnsley

A delightfully informal view of pupils from the old grammar school in Worsbrough village, from a picture postcard produced by George Washington Irving, posted in Barnsley on 25 July 1906. The message, to a Mrs Clayton of Whitley: 'I think you know a lot of children in this post card, With Love From Nellie.'

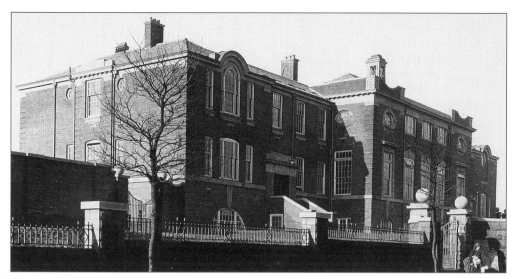

The New Barnsley Grammar School, a quality postcard produced by Lamb of Racecommon Road and sent from Cudworth post office to a Mrs Sharpe, Pontefract Road, Cudworth, in 1914. In 1887 Queen Victoria approved a parliamentary recommendation that the 300-year-old Archbishop Holgate Grammar School at Hemsworth was transferred to Barnsley with Mr R.H. Butler as Head of the amalgamated schools. In January 1912 the old Church Street School (now the town art gallery) was sold for £3,500 to Samuel Joshua Cooper and a new building erected on Shaw Lane. By 1913 the school had 207 pupils, inceasing to 424 boys after the First World War. As the Holgate School it is now a mixed comprehensive, but as an educational institution it reaches back five centuries, and probably to medieval times.

Barnsley Grammar School class, 1946–47. Back row, left to right: Marsden, Green, Smith, Rushton, Pyne and Mason. Middle row: Pearson, Winderbank, Millington, Elliott, Fairclough, Robinson, Boyden and Fitzpatrick. Front row: Pray, Chambers, Hulson, Mr Rusby, Pashley, Iverson and Hague. The photograph is included by courtesy of former member of the class Peter Grafton, who was absent on the day.

Hemingfield Ellis Church of England Infants' Standard 1 (1923–24) photographed by Mr J. Blackburn. Back row, left to right: Alan Swift, Colin Bell, George Middleton, Sydney Askin, Ronnie Knowles, Albert Fowler, Norman Harris, Joseph Cocking and Alan Morris. Fourth row: Annie Frost, Elizabeth Wray, Lily Holmes, Hilda Heeson, Elsie Tomlinson, Irene Middleton, Hilda Thickett and Grace Monaghan. Third row: Harry Lisles, Connie Kaye, Emily Spencer, Gwendoline Carter, Sybil Ward, Eliza Watkin, Annie James, Eliza Rodgers, Phyllis Rance and Morva Bailey. Second row: Edith Stenton, Kathleen Skews, Rose Robinson, Mary Parkin, Ida Blackburn (photographer's daughter), Ena Moore, Isa Eyre and Emma Beevors. Front row: Walter Stenton, Jack Rhodes, Jack Senior, Robert Allen, Albert Helliwell, Tom Lockwood, Harry Hunt and Roland Briggs. Class teacher was Miss Cook, who was also Headmistress of the infants' school.

Two former pupils shown on the 1923–24 class photograph, Mrs Grace Pollendine (née Monaghan) and Irene Moulds (née Middleton), had a happy reunion in February 1999 – after seventy-two years! Grace qualified as a Queen's District Nurse, working for the Barnsley Health Authority, while Irene became a nanny on leaving school, later working in a butcher's shop and for the Taylor family, printers, at Wombwell.

Class 3 at Hemmingfield Junior School, 1998 – an interesting contrast with the earlier photograph. Back row, left to right: Mr K. Oliver, Mrs K. Marshall, Kierian Williams, Adam Clarke, Ian Peters, Kerry Arnold, Kerry Wild, Rachael Whitehead, Rachael Kay and Mr S. Heald. Third row: Daniel Williams, Brendon Briggs, Joe Esberger, Emma Wake, Laura Wildman, Lauran Sheldon, Laura Dennis, Kaley Boldy, Lindsey Hoyland and Mrs M. Howarth. Second row: Craig Hardcastle, Ben Barber, Kelly Roebuck, Rachael Horbury, Jodie Glazzard, Jessica Allott, Joe Hallam, Adam Bourne and Luke Stevenson. Front row: Laura Davies, Kirstie Rawson, Rachel Lewis and Jason Bourne.

Boys' class at John Street School, Wombwell, 1918. Back row, left to right: Herbert Haller, an extremely cheerful Harold Hill, Ledberry, Thomas Basindale, Arthur Milburn, -?-, Thomas Owen, Jack Elliott. Middle row: Fowler, -?-, Godridge, Flint, Len Rothery, Alfred Jones, Guy Davies, Horace Crowther and Fred Scott. Front row: Frank Connelly, Fred Briggs, Newman, Horace Rook, John Harrison, Fowler, -?-, Leslie Payling and H. Winder. The school was demolished in 1997.

Harold Hill, still smiling on his ninetieth birthday in 1997.

Although no pupils have been identified on this school photograph at Hoyle Mill, *c.* 1910, it serves as an interesting social document. Many would be children of glassworkers and miners. There was no school uniform, but mothers went to great pains in order to kit sons and daughters in their Sunday best for such occasions. The children had to stand or sit still, probably for several minutes, hardly a cheerful proposition, so there aren't too many smiles, apart from the teacher and the girl she is 'supporting'. The girl given the responsibility of holding the information slate appears to be finding the task a great strain.

Older children, about ten years old, are shown on this photograph of Class 7xc at Higham Church of England School, *c.* 1920. The 'x' was apparently used to identify a 'brighter' year group but there are only six girls out of twenty-three. Back row, left to right: Herbert Woller, -?-, Fred Swainson and Mr Woodcock. Middle row: Charlie Wormald, Stanley Green, Tommy Jukes, George Ward (just behind Tom), Edwin Robinson, Willis Watkinson, Wilf Harris, -?-, Gerald Booth, George Elvin and Donald Hanks. Front row: Jack Marsh, Walter Lucas, Fearn, Mary Whitehead, Edna Speight, Winnie Scholey, Alice Jackson and Edith Charlesworth.

A scene from a production of *Macbeth* (act one, scene two) performed by Barnsley Grammar School in March 1947. Left to right: Irwin (as Donaldbain), Brammer (Duncan), Hitchen (Lennox), Rigby (Malcolm) and Peter Grafton (Sergeant).

This delightful photograph by Irvin Harris of a group of children by the wall of 83 Dearne Hall Road, at Lower Barugh, is believed to have been taken in the summer of 1947. The building in the background, beyond the bridge, is the former St Andrew's Mission Church. Back row, left to right: Billy Shaw, John Smith, Gary Sunderland, Jackie Ward, Eric Thompson, Edward Broadbent, Elsie Smith and Elaine Broadbent. Front row: Jean Schofield, Trevor Ward, -?-, Dennis Smith, Mary Carter, Geoffrey Ward, Irene Turner, Ethel Porter, June Turner, Ann Sanders, Pauline Scattergood (with a younger sister?), Pearl Wilks, and Doreen Ward. The boy with his hands in his pockets at the front is Malcolm Broadbent. Several attended a reunion at the nearby Miller's Arms on Saturday 17 April 1999. *Harris Collection*

Barnsley Girls' High School, shortly after its opening on 22 November 1909; it was built at a cost of £25,000. The school had functioned for four years in premises on Queens Road. The first headmistress, the formidable Miss A.J. Robinson, was appointed on a salary of £300 a year, presiding over 167 girls, 60 of whom were pupil-teachers, until her retirement in 1913. Her staff were paid £90–100 a year.

In more informal times, but with compulsory uniform, this is art teacher Miss Dora Haigh with a small group of pupils at the Barnsley Girls' High School, c. 1960. Her sister, Lucy Irene, taught at Longcar Central School while brother Edwin was Head of Barnsley School of Art where he taught for more than fifty years.

Agnes Road Boys' School, Barnsley (Standard 2a), 1924. Judging by their smart attire the boys were probably given notice of the impending photographer's visit; Scholastic Photo Specialists of Hartlepool probably had a contract or agreement with the local education authority. Of the forty-eight lads a number are believed to be as follows: Back row, left to right: (second) Arthur Dearden, (fifth) Frank Mead and (eleventh) John Laughton. Middle row: (sixth) Whittaker, (ninth) Philip Windmill and (twelfth) Stephton; the teacher was Mrs Hesp. Front row: (fifteenth) Robert Austin and (sixteenth) Guest.

May (b. 1918, shown on the St Mary's infants' photograph on p. 59) and Arthur Dearden (b. 1915, who attended Agnes Road Boys' – he is on the photograph above – and Longcar School), shown here in 1999, met at Shaw Lane Cricket Club and married in 1941. Arthur trained to be a teacher in 1939 with short spells at Littleworth and Longcar Schools before army service intervened. After the war he taught handicrafts at Mark Street School from 1946 to 1966. The couple, who have two great grandchildren, are due to celebrate their diamond wedding anniversary in 2001. Arthur recalls that as a boy he enjoyed visiting Barnsley's October Fair at Churchfield, buying licorice sticks and pomegranates.

Longcar School, autumn 1927. Back row, left to right: (first) ? Larkin, (third) Stanley Blenkinsop. Fourth row: (first) Marie Mannas, (third) Burton, (fourth) R. Smith, (fifth) Arthur Dearden. Third row: (second) Fransworth. Second row: (fourth) James Bretton, (seventh) Donald Mathewman. Front row: (second) Hammond, (third) Balliol. The staff are L.S. Felkin and G.H. Turner.

St Mary's C of E Infants', Barnsley, 1923. Back row, left to right: (fourth) Donald Potter. Third row: (fourth) Muriel Walshaw, (sixth) Joan Dunk, (seventh) Hilda Thorpe, (ninth) May Foster. Second row: (eleventh) Gwennie Rushforth. Front row: (first) Thomas Watling, (third) Doris Williams and (fourth) Donald Greathead (both holding slate).

Senior girls (thirteen and fourteen year olds) at Mapplewell School, *c.* 1933. They would soon be leaving school, many to find work in local factories, in service or helping to look after younger brothers and sisters. Very few if any would have any further education. The author's mother, Agnes Stone, is on the back row, sixth from the left; she found employment in the household of a local doctor.

A party involving the reception class at Shawlands Primary School, Shaw Lane, Barnsley (headmaster Mr D. Lycett), photographed by the author on Wednesday 23 July 1986 in celebration of the marriage of Prince Andrew and Sarah Ferguson (Duke and Duchess of York). Many of these children will now be in further and higher education.

CHAPTER FOUR

PITS, PEOPLE & POLITICS

Explosions at the Oaks Colliery on 11–12 December 1866 caused the deaths of 361 men and boys, including a team of volunteer rescue workers, and remains England's worst mining disaster. The impact on small communities such as Hoyle Mill was immense with virtually every household affected, leaving more than 100 widows and about 350 orphaned children. The photograph shows the widow of Thomas Hyde, still wearing mourning clothes about fifty years later, holding a prayer book. The body of her husband, a pit-sinker, was recovered eighteen months after the disaster. Mrs Hyde identified him from a patch that she had sewn on his trousers. The couple, both aged twenty-five, with two young children, had just moved into the area from Derbyshire. It serves as a telling reminder of one of the most tragic periods in Barnsley's history.

The so-called Oaks Monument at the crest of Kendray Hill, its rear overlooking the site of the ill-fated colliery. This postcard dates from 1919, six years after the monument was belatedly erected courtesy of businessman Samuel Joshua Cooper. It was 'a tribute to the memory of Parkin Jeffcock and other heroes of the rescue parties' and the 'single bravery' of John Edward Mammatt and Thomas William Embleton who rescued 'the sole survivor'. There is no mention of the lost miners, some buried in a mass grave in Ardsley churchyard, and many more entombed in the pit.

The Oaks Monument statue (*Gloria Victus*) was restored by Sheffield sculpture Chris Bolton in 1992, but in 1998 it had to undergo more detailed and expensive repair at Sheffield Hallam University after vandals had knocked it off its plinth and broken part of the angel's wing. The statue, seen here with Barnsley Council's Paul Gorman just before its re-erection, was also restored to its former golden glory. *Wes Hobson*

A Gothard postcard commemorating a horrific accident at Barrow Colliery, Worsbrough Dale, on Friday 15 November 1907, when seven men were killed and nine others injured. Isaac Farrer's mother was preparing his twenty-first birthday tea at the time while Tom Cope (twenty-three), whose father had been killed at Swaithe Main Colliery sixteen years earlier, was engaged to be married; and Byas Rooke (twenty-two) had stopped to talk to a friend rather than take the previous ascent with his brother. Walter Goodchild left a widow and six children. The seven men were flung out of a double-decker, open-fronted cage which was still attached to a landing when winding commenced. There were many emotional scenes at the pit-head on the Friday night. One young miner rushed to the cabin where the bodies were placed and asked to see one of them. Bursting into tears, he knelt and kissed the uncovered face of his best mate. They had been working together that same afternoon.

The South Yorkshire Miners' Association was formed in 1858 when sixty-two men from twenty-six pits met on two occasions at the Old White Bear Inn, Shambles Street (on a site now occupied by Barnsley's Central Library), pictured here in the early 1900s.

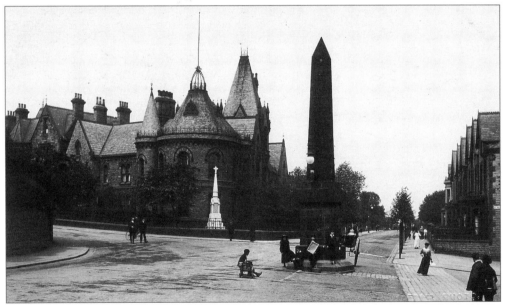

The distinctive miners' offices opened in 1874 and cost £8,000 to build, one of the first purpose-built trade union headquarters in the country. It was described by Secretary John Normansell as having 'a cheerful and pleasant appearance', though he also spoke about the dreadful working conditions, injuries and loss of life that wrecked so many mining families. The junction (Huddersfield Road/Old Mill Lane/Victoria Road) and the Mence Obelisk (demolished in 1931) was a popular viewpoint for Edwardian photographers.

IN MEMORY OF
THOSE WHO HAVE LOST THEIR LIVES
IN SUPPORTING THEIR UNION
IN TIMES OF STRUGGLE

Standing outside the National Union of Mineworkers' premises is a superb sculpture by Graham Ibberson showing a miner and his family. It was commissioned in 1993.

This remarkable photograph, dating from 1912, shows coal-pickers and their families at Silkstone, a fascinating social document of the strike. *Old Barnsley*

Many striking miners defied danger during the long 1984–85 strike, digging coal from recently uncovered old workings behind Shaw Lane cricket club and off Broadway.

Issuing bread from the Providence Club, Darfield, 1920s, one of a series of excellent mining photographs taken by R.J. Short of Wombwell.

Boys enjoying a swim during the 1926 lock-out at Low Valley, near Darfield. *R.J. Short*

Irvin Harris (1912–98) was a miner and pit deputy working mainly at Woolley Colliery but also at Barrow. He was a keen photographer too, undertaking commissions for weddings, schools, football teams and so on, but his underground mining photographs are of great interest and high quality. This surreptitious self-portrait dates from about 1937, showing him shovelling coal ten years before nationalisation. Having to rely on light from cap and oil lamps and a slow (100 ASA) film meant estimating an exposure which could range from one to five minutes. He used a Super Baldina folding camera with an F4.5 lens, but wasn't officially allowed to take photographs underground until August 1939. *Harris Collection*

Town Clerk Mr A.E. Gillfillan, Prime Minister and Mrs Clement Attlee, Mayor Charles Bentley and (extreme right) Minister of Power Emmanuel ('Manny') Shinwell pose for photographs on the steps of Barnsley Town Hall on the morning of Saturday 21 June 1947. They were in town to address a mass demonstration of miners in Locke Park. People in the background include Arthur Horner, NUM General Secretary (third from left, partly obscured) and on the extreme right Lord Citrine (Walter McLennan) of the new National Coal Board.

Irvin Harris photographed miners enjoying the new pit-head baths at Woolley Colliery. They opened in August 1939 but Joe Hall, President of the Yorkshire Miners, referred to one of his favourite subjects: the ritual and advantages of bathing in a tin bath. No doubt there were men who preferred to carry their 'badge of courage' home (in fact some thought that washing weakened the back and coaldust healed cuts), but increasingly the pit was the place to leave work muck. *Harris Collection*

A fine study by Irvin Harris of coal-cutting at Woolley Colliery, 1948. The man on the left is believed to be a Mr Trainer who lived at Smithies. *Harris Collection*

A pit deputy making notes via the light from his cap lamp – another excellent photograph by Irvin Harris, taken at Barrow Colliery in January 1951. *Harris Collection*

Underground pit pony stalls at Woolley Colliery, *c.* 1950. The cat was an essential asset for keeping down vermin. From 1911 horse-keepers had to keep a record of their animals (each one named), their condition and daily movement. During the 1921 strike, pit pony races were staged in the big field between Darfield and Ardsley on 16 June in aid of the miners' distress fund. The pony Doctor won the 'derby'. Ponies from Dearne Valley, Houghton Main and Mitchell Main took part in events such as the Snape Hill Stakes and Darfield St Leger. There are many amusing anecdotes concerning pit ponies, including one where Bruce ate a miner's false teeth which had been wrapped in paper, placed in his jacket pocket and hung up. The pony had a reputation for gobbling 'snap' at any opportunity at Darfield Main! *Harris Collection*

Coal tubs underground at Barrow Colliery, January 1951. *Harris Collection*

A pit deputy communicating with the surface by telephone, Woolley Colliery, Thorncliffe North Side (Airway), 1972. *Harris Collection*

Shot-firing at Woolley Colliery, Silkstone Seam, 1952. In recent years vibration white finger has become a recognised industrial disease, due to the long-term use of powerful drills in the shot-firing process. *Harris Collection*

Roy Mason in his pit clothes on the back steps of his home at 292 Carlton Road, Smithies, *c*. 1950. He started work at Wharncliffe Woodmoor 4/5 Colliery at the age of fourteen in 1938, becoming a fitter and even obtaining his deputy certificate, although he never functioned in this capacity. His early working experiences undoubtedly shaped his trade union and political interests. Mr Mason was buried in underground accidents on three occasions but by the age of twenty-three was representing his fellow miners via the union branch committee, and served as a Yorkshire NUM delegate only two years later.

Roy Mason on the terrace of the House of Commons in 1953, with Horace Holmes (and wife), the Hemsworth member and Yorkshire Whip who introduced him to the House. Following the retirement of Sydney Schofield, Roy had gained the confidence and support of the Yorkshire Miners Parliamentary Panel and the local Labour Party, entering the Commons on 31 March at the age of twenty-nine as Barnsley's youngest-ever MP.

George Brown, First Secretary of State for Economic Affairs in the Labour Government, speaking at the Yorkshire Miners' Gala and demonstration, Locke Park, Saturday 19 June 1965. He was photographed by the author.

The leading party at the 1969 Yorkshire miners' demonstration walk along Church Street; the Yorkshire NUM offices are in the background. They include, left to right, Jack Leigh (Yorkshire miners' Vice President), Rt Hon. Roy Mason MP, Mrs Hinchcliffe and her husband, Ald. Theodore (Mayor) and Sydney Schofield (Yorkshire miners' General Secretary).

Roy Mason, MP and Minister of Power, addressing a large crowd at the miners' gala in Locke Park, 1969.

Michael Foot MP, then Secretary of State for Employment, stressing a point at the Yorkshire miners' gala in Locke Park, 1975.

A happy occasion for Roy Mason, who has the cheerful help of his family, wife Marjory and daughters Susan and Jill, helping to dispatch election addresses in 1959. The young MP had already made a considerable impact in the House of Commons and also 'at home' as a hard-working constituency representative. He was soon to be Labour front bench spokesman on post office affairs and, after the 1964 election, Minister of State at the Board of Trade.

Here, Roy Mason MP, soon to be appointed to the high office of Secretary of State for Defence by Harold Wilson, is surrounded by a sea of children from Longcar School, Racecommon Road, during the 1974 election campaign. He had previously demonstrated his abilities as Postmaster General (1968), Minister of Power (1968) and, with cabinet responsibility, President of the Board of Trade (1969–70) in the previous Labour Government.

During the 1970s Roy Mason (centre) made regular visits to Barnsley area pits, on this occasion to Dodworth with fellow MP (for Penistone) Allen McKay (left), the colliery manager and police protection officers.

Former Wharncliffe Silkstone miner and local historian Mr A.K. Clayton at Cortonwood Colliery, which was at the forefront of the 1984–85 strike, photographed by the author a few days after the pit was closed in May 1986. Shortly after this visit the surface buildings were hastily demolished. The shafts were capped in 1988.

Witty graffiti inscribed in chalk on one of Cortonwood's surface buildings. Walking around the site on a pleasant early summer's day was both an eerie and sad experience.

An estimated 4–5,000 people packed into Barnsley town centre, even 'spilling over' the balcony of the Metropolitan Centre on Cheapside, on Saturday 7 November 1992 in protest at the Tory Government's plan to close thirty-one collieries. Speakers included the Bishop of Wakefield, the Rt Rev. Nigel McCulloch, and NUM President Arthur Scargill. The event was even attended by Ukrainian cosmonaut Alexander Volkov from Barnsley's twin town Gorlovka.

A 'Save Our Pits' sticker on the forehead of a small boy just about sums up the strength of feeling at the Fight for Coal Rally.

Barnsley's MP was appointed Secretary of State for Northern Ireland by James Callaghan in September 1976, and served until 1979; this was just one of seven major offices of state that he had held in his impressive career. In 1987 Roy Mason PC was honoured with a life peerage, after thirty-four years of parliamentary service. However, as Lord Mason of Barnsley he continues to be very active in the House of Lords and supports many local causes, but with the constant vigilance of police guards. He was photographed at his home by the author in 1999.

An interesting photograph of Wombwell Main Colliery by Lamb & Co., *c.* 1910; some miners are finishing their shift. The BBCS horse and cart appears to be delivering crates of mineral water to quench the miners' thirst.

The Rheolaveur Washery and Screening Plant at Darton Main Colliery, 1925. Its shafts were sunk in 1914–15 but the pit was apparently slow to develop until 1924, when the Strafford Collieries Co. Ltd took control, establishing a new estate of 200 houses next to the mine.

The Miners' Rest at Old Town, the ancient site of Barnsley, has a datestone of 1909, but replaced an earlier pub. It even has its own bowling green, leased (at a peppercorn rent) to the Old Town Bowling Club. The present (1999) licensee is Steph Griffiths, whose husband Dennis is landlord of the Grey Horse, just a car park away!

CHAPTER FIVE

SPORTING TIMES

Tommy Taylor, pictured here in cartoon format as a Manchester United player, was one of eight 'Busby Babes' killed in the Munich disaster on 6 February 1958, when he was regarded as one of the best centre-forwards in the world. Born at Smithies in 1932, Tommy played for his local amateur team before being recruited to Barnsley FC's ground-staff, playing a few games for the first team while undergoing National Service, turning professional in May 1952. He made forty-four appearances for the club, scoring twenty-six goals before his record £29,999 transfer to Old Trafford on 4 March 1953. Manchester United had agreed to pay £30,000 but Busby gave a pound to the Oakwell tea lady, protecting the 21-year-old from the responsibility of a £30,000 price tag. The maximum wage was £15 a week. Taylor scored 112 First Division goals from only 166 appearances for United, won two championship medals and played in the 1957 Cup Final. He made nineteen England appearances, scoring fourteen times, including two hat-tricks. What price and wages would he command today? Plaques celebrating the achievements of Tommy and Wombwell-born Mark Jones who was also killed at Munich were unveiled at Oakwell and Darfield Foulstone School in 1998, forty years after the tragedy.

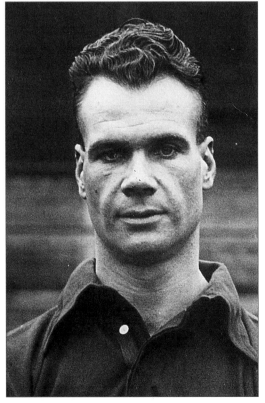

Barnsley FC only finished fifteenth in Division 2 in the season 1950/51 despite the brilliance of Cec McCormack (signed from non-league Chelmsford) who scored thirty-three goals from thirty-seven appearances. Back row, left to right: Danny Blanchflower, Herbert Glover, Eddie Bannister, Pat Kelly, Gordon Pallister and Jimmy Baxter. Front row: Gavin Smith, Eddie McMorran, Cec McCormack, Tommy Taylor and Johnny Kelly.

Arthur Glover (1918–98) joined Barnsley FC as a semi-professional from Regent Street 'Congs' in March 1935. His first-team debut was against Stockport County in January 1938. Despite the intervening war years Arthur, a versatile and strong defensive player, made 193 first team appearances over eighteen seasons. He was also a boxer, accomplished cricketer and in later life, along with brother Ronnie, a keen cyclist.

SECOND DIVISION.

Date	Opponent		F	A
1950				
Aug. 19	Southampton	h	1	2
24	Hull City	a	3	3
26	Chesterfield	a	2	1
30	Hull City	a	4	2
Sept. 2	Sheffield United	h	2	0
6	Brentford	h	2	3
9	Luton Town	a	2	1
13	Brentford	a	2	0
16	Leeds United	a	2	2
23	West Ham United	h	1	2
30	Swansea Town	a	0	1
Oct. 7	Grimsby Town	h	3	1
14	Birmingham City	a	4	2
21	Preston North End	h	4	1
28	Notts County	a	1	2
Nov. 4	Queens Park Rangers	h	7	0
11	Bury	a	3	0
18	Cardiff City	h	0	0
25	Coventry City	a	3	3
Dec. 2	Manchester City	h	1	1
9	Preston N. E.	a	2	0
16	Southampton	a	0	1
23	Chesterfield	h		
25	Doncaster Rovers	a		
26	Doncaster Rovers	h		
30	Sheffield United	h		
1951				
Jan. 1	—			
6	Northampton T.—3rd Rnd	a		
13	Luton Town	a		
20	Leeds United	h		
27	F.A. Cup 4th Round			
Feb. 3	West Ham United	a		
10	F.A. Cup 5th Round			
17	Swansea Town	h		
24	Grimsby Town	a		
Mar. 3	Birmingham City	h		
10	Preston North End	a		
17	Notts County	h		
23	Blackburn Rovers	a		
24	Queens Park Rangers	a		
26	Blackburn Rovers	h		
31	Bury	h		
Apl. 7	Cardiff City	a		
14	Coventry City	h		
21	Manchester City	a		
28	Leicester City	h		

CENTRAL LEAGUE

Date	Opponent		F	A
1950				
Aug. 19	Blackburn R. Res.	a	0	2
23	Blackpool Res.	h	1	2
26	Chesterfield Res.	h	1	2
Sept. 2	Sheffield Utd. Res.	a	2	4
9	Manchester Utd. Res.	a	0	1
11	Liverpool Res.	h	1	3
16	Leeds United Res.	a	1	1
20	Liverpool	h	0	1
23	Aston Villa Res.	h	1	2
30	Wolverhampton Res.	h	0	3
Oct. 7	Sheffield Wed. Res.	a	2	3
14	Manchester City Res.	h	3	3
21	Newcastle Utd. Res.	h	0	2
28	West Brom Res.	h	2	1
Nov. 4	Huddersfield T. Res.	a	1	1
11	Stoke City Res.	h	3	1
18	Everton Res.	h	3	2
25	Bury Reserves	h	1	0
Dec. 2	Burnley Res.	a	1	0
9	Preston N. E. Res.	h		
16	Blackburn R. Res.	h		
23	Chesterfield Res.	a		
23	Derby County Res.	h		
26	Derby County Res.	a		
30	Sheffield United Res.	a		
1951				
Jan. 1	—			
6	—			
13	Manchester U. Res.	h		
20	Leeds United Res.	a		
27	—			
Feb. 3	Aston Villa Res.	h		
10	—			
17	Wolverhampton Res.	a		
24	Sheffield Wed. Res.	h		
Mar. 3	Manchester C. Res.	a		
10	Newcastle U. Res.	h		
17	West Brom Res.	a		
23	Bolton W. Res.	a		
26	—			
31	Stoke City Res.	a		
Apl. 7	Everton Res.	h		
14	Bury Reserves	h		
21	Burnley Res.	h		
28	Preston N. E. Res.	a		
May 5	Bolton W. Res.	h		

SECOND DIVISION.

	P	W	L	D	F	A	Pts.
Manchester C	21	11	4	6	49	34	28
Coventry C.	22	12	7	3	46	26	27
Southampton	22	11	6	5	33	33	27
Birmingham	22	11	7	4	37	28	26
Blackburn	22	11	7	4	34	32	26
Barnsley	22	10	7	5	49	29	25
Preston N.E.	22	11	8	3	43	30	25
Cardiff City	21	7	4	10	27	21	24
Hull City	21	8	6	7	39	32	23
West Ham	21	10	8	3	36	37	23
Sheffield U.	21	8	7	6	39	32	22
Doncaster R.	21	7	6	8	31	33	22
Notts County	21	7	8	6	39	32	20
Leeds United	21	7	8	6	35	31	20
Leicester C.	21	7	8	6	32	31	20
Chesterfield	22	5	9	8	26	37	18
Queens P. R.	22	7	10	4	34	47	18
Brentford	22	7	11	4	28	48	18
Bury	21	7	10	4	25	36	16
Swansea T.	21	7	12	2	30	45	16
Grimsby T.	21	4	11	6	37	54	14
Luton Town	21	3	12	6	21	36	12

Up to and including Sat. Dec. 16th.

CENTRAL LEAGUE

	P	W	L	D	F	A	Pts.
Wolves Res.	22	18	4	0	63	12	36
Aston V. Rs.	22	13	6	3	37	24	29
Huddersfield	21	11	4	7	35	29	29
Blackpool R.	21	9	3	9	34	21	27
West B. Res.	22	9	4	9	39	33	27
Liverpool Rs.	22	11	7	4	29	24	26
Preston Res.	21	10	6	5	40	27	25
Burnley Res.	22	9	6	7	31	21	25
Newcastle Rs.	21	9	6	6	35	25	24
Manch. C. Rs.	21	10	7	4	47	36	24
Bolton Res.	21	8	5	5	31	38	21
Sheffield W R	21	6	8	7	33	37	19
Everton Res.	19	7	7	5	36	43	19
Sheffield U R	20	6	8	6	30	27	18
Manch. U. R.	21	6	9	6	31	35	18
Bury Res.	21	7	10	4	30	41	18
Leeds Res.	22	6	11	5	24	35	17
Blackburn R	21	6	11	4	30	46	16
Barnsley Res.	21	4	11	6	25	39	14
Derby Res.	21	5	13	3	36	42	13
Chesterf'ld R.	21	3	11	7	17	46	13
Stoke C. Rs.	21	2	15	4	17	49	8

Up to and including Sat. Dec. 16th.

BARNSLEY (Red Shirts, White Knickers).   Kick-of 2-15

1
R   KELLY, P.   L

2   3
BANNISTER   PALLISTER

4   5   6
BLANCHFLOWER   GLOVER   NORMANTON

7   8   9   10   11
SMITH McMORRAN McCORMACK   TAYLOR KELLY, J.

11   10   9   8   7
MARTIN LAWLOR   TINDILL DOHERTY CALVERLEY

6   4
MILLER   BYCROFT   JONES

3   2
GRAHAM   HAINSWORTH

1
L   HARDWICK   R

DONCASTER ROVERS (White Shirts, Black Shorts)

Teams printed in the official Barnsley FC programme for Boxing Day 1950. A crowd of 33,867 attended the fixture against local rivals Doncaster Rovers who 'did the double', winning 1–0 at Oakwell after a 3–2 victory at Belle Vue on Christmas Day.

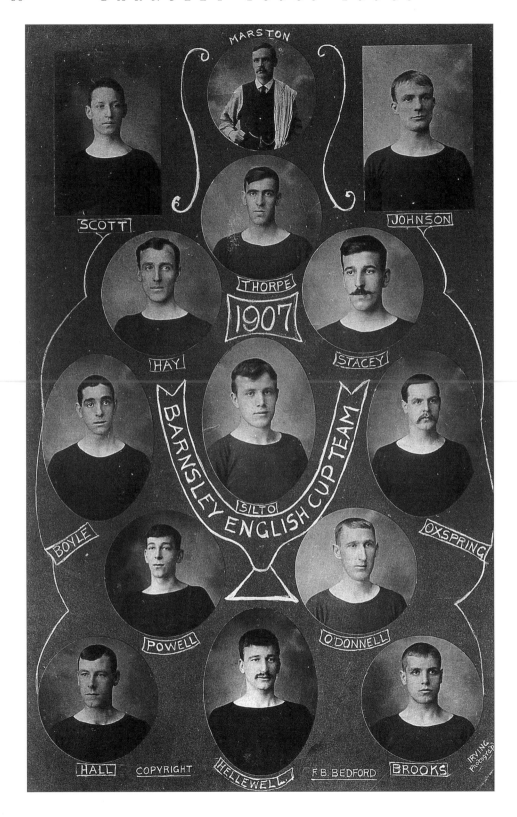

Barnsley FC, relegated after their first season in the Premiership, parade at the start of season 1998/99. Back row, left to right: Hristov, Moses, Markstedt, O'Callaghan, de Zeew, Fjortoft, Ward, van Der Laan, Kennedy, Bassinder and Jones. Middle row: Walker (youth coach), Smith (P., physio), Winstanley (coach), Krizan, Tinkler, Morgan, Sadler, Peese, Watson, Bullock (A), Rose, McClare, Smith (A), Gregory, Tarmey (physio) and Shirtliff (assistant manager). Front row: Heckingbottom, Marcelle, Appleby, Bagshaw, Richardson, Hendrie (player-manager), Liddell, Bullock (M), Barnard, Eaden and Sheridan. It was a disappointing season but the club did reach the FA Cup quarter finals, losing at Oakwell to a wonderful individual goal from Tottenham's most flamboyant player, David Ginola. *Wes Hobson*

Opposite: This montage (by George Washington Irving) celebrates Barnsley FC's first appearance in the quarter-final of the FA Cup in 1907 when they were defeated 0–1 at Oakwell by Woolwich Arsenal before a record crowd of 13,871. The players earned £1–£3 per week. Centre-half Tommy Boyle, signed from Platts Common in 1906, was captain during the magnificent cup run of 1909/10 when the Reds reached the final for the first time. He was a class player but was controversially sold to Burnley, where he gained international caps, for £1,250 in 1911.

A series of postcards were issued in 1910 by Irving and Randall in celebration of Barnsley's first FA Cup appearance, several featuring Amos, the comic mascot, shown here outside the club headquarters, the Clarence Hotel, Sheffield Road. In 1912 the FA cup was on display here, following Second Division Barnsley's remarkable victory over West Brom and coinciding with the visit of King George V. The Barnsley players were said to have each received £25 for winning the cup – and a commemorative snuff box! *Old Barnsley*

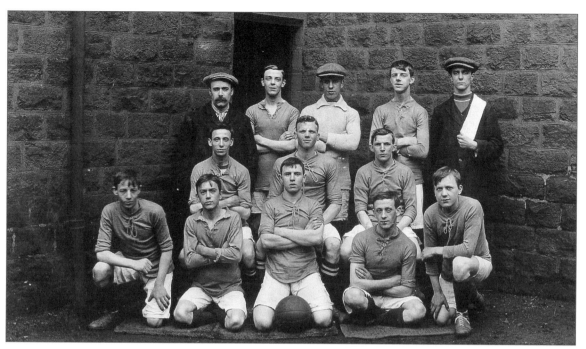

Before the outbreak of the First World War there were many amateur teams in the Barnsley area. Some claimed to represent particular streets and pubs; others, churches, chapels, pits and works. Here we see a carefully arranged (goalie and full-backs, half-backs and forwards) Cornstalk's FC, perhaps inspired by the excitement of 1912.

A slightly more informal example, taken before a game, showing Farrer Street Congregational FC, *c.* 1910.

Albert Street FC, 1906/7. For some early teams a visit to a professional studio was the best way to ensure a team photograph, but one or two of the lads appear to have forgotten their kit.

The young lads of Darfield Athletic had a smart kit, but the goalkeeper is not easy to identify.

A remarkable amateur football match took place at the Dearne ground behind the Tollgate Hotel, Wakefield Road, in 1937, when Regent Street Congregation and Ward Green met in the Junior Cup final. The 'Congs' were down 0–4 after thirty minutes but finished the game winning 6–5. Back row, left to right: Harrison Barrowclough, Fred Elliott (goalkeeper) and Gough. Middle row: half-backs Oscar Hold (who went on to manage Cambridge City, Doncaster Rovers and several international sides), Frank Bedford and McPhearson (scorer). Front row, forwards Frank Porter (scorer), T. Bartlam (scored a hat-trick), F. Shaw, H. Brook, George Heppleston (scorer). The photograph which also shows 'officials' was taken at the reception.

Barnsley FC, champions of Division 3 (North), had an exceptionally good team in 1938/39, the last full season before the outbreak of war, scoring ninety-four goals and winning thirty games, finishing way ahead of second-placed Doncaster Rovers. Back row, left to right: Beaumont Asquith (who scored twenty-eight goals and then was sold to Manchester United), N. Brunskill, C. Binns, J. Everest and J. Calder. Third row: T. Ratcliffe (trainer), F. Bokas, J. Steele, J. Lang, B. Shotton and manager Angus Seed. Second row: J. Logan, G. Tomlinson (chairman), B. Harper (captain), J. Richards (vice-chairman) and E. Williams. Front row: G. Bullock and D. McGarry.

Barnsley Rugby Union Club, 1924/25, when they played in a field on Cockerham Lane, photographed by Denton & Co. Back row, left to right: B.M. Newman, C. Boseley, C. Dodgson, J.M. Bell, D.S. Southcombe, R.M. Beaman, I. Lunn, J.E. Wainwright and the Rev. R. Huggard (president). Front row: E.T. Griffiths, J.T. Lunn, F. Elliston, E.H. Umbers (captain and MD of Barnsley Brewery), G.L. Stirling (secretary), F.J. Askham and A.L. McPhail.

The Rev. Richard Huggard had founded the Barnsley Rugby Union Club in 1902. He was vicar at St John's Church, Duke Street (now demolished) and chaplain to the 'Barnsley Pals', therefore responsible for 'swearing in' many men who joined the 13/14th Battalions of the York and Lancaster Regiment. His youngest son, 2nd Lieutenant L.D.R. Huggard, was killed in France by shell fragments.

Keeping racing pigeons – usually 'homers' but also 'milers' – was (and still remains in some areas) a popular interest in mining communities. Here we can see my grandfather, Fred Elliott (1887–1948) outside his allotment loft in the village of Carlton in the 1940s.

Cawthorne village cricket team, photographed by Rowland Wilkinson at the Miners' Welfare ground, off Tivydale (Dark Lane), 1936. Back row, left to right: E. Lisle, Harry Fish (who became Mayor of Barnsley), Charlie Hopton, Jack Fish, J. Buckley, F. Buckley and E. Fish. Front row: R. Fish, C.A. Buckley, Noel F. Moxon (village historian and musician), F. Lisle, R. Midgley and C. MacNaught. *Chris Moxon Collection*

Postmaster Rowland Wilkinson at the door of his Cawthorne premises, *c.* 1908. 'The famous Elswick Cycle' is illustrated on the large hoarding, ranging in price from £6 15s 0d to £21; and there were plenty of bicycles, spare tyres and wheels on show. Here motorists could buy 'Pratt's Spirit' (petrol) in 2-gallon drums. Also note the picture postcards. Rowland, a very able photographer, produced many topographical views, including examples printed by local professionals such as Gothard and Lamb; and publishers such as Haigh Bros. *Old Barnsley*

Lord Mason of Barnsley, PC, the pit boy who became a peer, with Barnsley's famous umpire, Harold 'Dickie' Bird, in the House of Lords, 23 May 1988. The two friends are holding a picture relating to Dickie's 100th international appearance at Lords for the England versus West Indies match. When duties allow, Lord Mason has a great interest in outdoor sports such as golf and fishing, and of course supporting his home town football club.

Interior of Race Street swimming baths, *c.* 1907. In August 1874, shortly after its opening, 'Professor Marquis Bibbero gave an entertainment illustrative of useful and ornamental swimming, in the Corporation Baths', performing twenty-two 'feats'. New baths were added in 1914 (now demolished), but the old baths building remains as a Grade II listed structure, though it closed for swimming in 1989 when the Metrodome Leisure Centre opened.

Many swimming contests were held in the old baths. Barnsley Swimming Club was formed in 1878, while the Borough Police Life Saving Team were regular participants, as can be seen by the Award of Merit winners recorded by Irving in 1912. The group includes former town baker Samuel Marsland (seated, in costume on right of the photograph).

Barnsley's Tarzan? W.G. Modley described himself as a
'physical culture expert', teaching 'gymnastics, fencing,
self-defence, etc.' from his George Yard premises, off
Market Hill. W.G.'s son was Albert Modley
(1891–1979), the popular flat-capped comedian.

Anyone for tennis? Miss Mary Howard (b. 1922) had
her studio photograph taken in Barnsley in August
1938. Tennis was a popular summer sport for women.
A month earlier American Helen Wills Moody had won
the Wimbledon singles title for a record eighth time,
but in 1934 Britain won both the men's and women's
championships (Fred Perry and Dorothy Rounds).

This studio photograph by Will Randall shows Herbert Glover (1888–1949), a miner and a professional boxer – the 'Pitman's Champion', *c.* 1908. Born at the Three Travellers Inn, Shambles Street, where his father John was publican, Herbert later lived at Pogmoor and Wilthorpe. His son Arthur had a couple of professional bouts but, as we have already seen, had a highly successful career as a Barnsley footballer.

From 1974 until recent years Barnsley was one of the premier road racing towns in the country. Initiated and hosted by Barnsley Road Runners, the most famous event was the annual 'Barnsley Six' which, despite two tough circuits of the town, attracted hundreds of entrants from fun runners to top international athletes. Here the leading club runners dash along Shambles Street, just after the mass start of the men's race (in front of the Town Hall) in 1979. Just ahead of them was a long ascent up Racecommon Road, but a lap was not completed until an even harder climb up Old Mill Lane. The winner was Birchfield Harrier and Olympian Ray Smedley, in a time of 30.30 but every finisher, from youngsters of eighteen to veterans over seventy, received a commemorative certificate.

Cover of the 1979 programme. During the early years there were also races for boys, youths and women, and 'The Six' was celebrated by eagerly awaited supplements produced by the sports department of the *Barnsley Chronicle*, recording the name and time of every finisher.

Family fun runs were also very popular, raising money for a variety of charities. This one took place in Locke Park on Sunday 17 August 1986 during the Newsagents' Gala. Participants included Hannah and Natalie Elliott (aged two and five).

CHAPTER SIX

ENTERTAINMENT & EXCURSIONS

About twenty ladies (and one baby) wait outside the Marlborough Hotel, Dodworth Road, on board an open charabanc. Traditionally carriers operated from inns: the Marlborough was not a regular stopping place, but perhaps landlord Henry Simmons had organised the outing. A small crowd of well-wishers add interest to the scene, captured by Lamb in 1908. The driver has a rueful expression, his front seat passengers perhaps the most senior and formidable of the party. Note the array of hats, well pinned for the rush of air during such excursions. With solid tyres and a 20mph speed limit, journeys were long and uncomfortable.

George Booker's hire cars and charabancs were driven by brothers William, Harry, Herman and George. The Booker family progressed from operating horse-drawn carriages to running the first motorised public services route from their Millstone Inn, Peel Street (subsequently demolished and replaced by the Bookers Hotel, later named the King George Hotel and now Kingsley's) to Barugh Green and Cawthorne. *Old Barnsley*

Young children do well to contain their excitement, assembled in front of their mothers before a school coach trip apparently to Derbyshire, *c.* 1950. The excursion was organised for Park Road, Worsbrough Bridge, infants. *Old Barnsley*

180

GEORGE BOOKER LTD

TAXI CABS

PHONE DAY AND NIGHT

Clean, Smart and Reliable Cars
for Private Commercial & Professional Use
for Hire on the most Reasonable Terms.

MOTOR CHAR-A-BANCS

well appointed and up-to-date with
thoroughly experienced drivers.

TOURS FOR ANY DISTANCE ARRANGED.

Write for Specimen Routes and Fares.

We have numerous Testimonials for long distance trips.

MOTOR TRANSIT.

Motor Lorries for the quick transit of Goods, Merchandise, etc.,
direct from your works to destination.   Rates on application.

Execute your deliveries by the quickest method.

GEO. BOOKER LTD.,
Peel Street.

Telephone 271 (Two Lines).   Telegrams: "Motors, Barnsley."

This advertisement appeared in a Barnsley almanac of 1908. Motorised cabs had been introduced to London only five years earlier. Booker's operated from Peel Square (by Graham's Orchard) during the 1930s and early 1940s before their business was taken over by Barnsley British Co-operative Society.

By 1920 public motorised transport had become more luxurious and more numerous, family firms operating from out-of-town locations. This Greenhow Brothers vehicle, standing outside Middlewood Hall, Darfield, could probably accommodate twenty passengers, including those wishing to sit in the open next to the driver! The roof area, designed for luggage, was reached by rear stairs. *Old Barnsley*

This Talbot motor car must have turned a few heads as it passed through the streets of Barnsley and district during the early postwar years. Owning a private car was not beyond the reach of some ordinary families. It was only after 1931 that drivers were required to take driving or eyesight tests.

'Some Barnsley naturalists on a country ramble!' formed part of a handwritten caption to this picture postcard, posted at Boroughbridge on 13 July 1918. Maybe they were members of the Barnsley Naturalist Society, but their sartorial appearance, especially the ladies and their flamboyant hats, seems more appropriate to Ascot than country walking.

A crowded Locke Park paddling pool and children's play area on a warm summer's day, *c.* 1950. Public parks, initially founded by local benefactors as natural retreats in urban environments, were transformed by councils which gradually introduced a variety of additional attractions, including paddling and boating ponds. The photographer has done well to capture the atmosphere of this busy and evocative scene. *Old Barnsley*

Locke Park Pavilion Tearooms and staff, shortly after its grand opening in 1911. The Council had struggled to fund the £510 building costs but for many years it was a popular facility, exceptionally busy during summer Sundays, on gala days and at miners' demonstrations; and was even used for wedding receptions. In recent decades repeated vandalism and declining park use placed the building at risk. Fortunately the café was given a new lease of life in the summer of 1998, with tenants who were determined to restore it to its former glory.

Brass bands were in such great demand that bandstands were included in the sales catalogues of ironmasters. The Locke Park bandstand was produced by the Lion Foundry Company of Kirkintilloch, Scotland, at a cost of £326. An estimated crowd of 25,000 attended its official opening in 1908. Spectators are less numerous on this Edwardian picture postcard – and the grass appears to be in need of mowing!

Bandmaster Arthur Kelk, baton held in his right hand and watch-chain heavy with medals, stands proudly behind a large trophy and plaque, from a postcard on 26 August 1907. Around him are an assortment of miners, millworkers and glassworkers who formed the Barnsley Borough Town Band. The occasion celebrated their success at the prestigious National Brass Band Festival at Crystal Palace. Any band that won a prize there was bound to be good.

The Barnsley National Reserve Band serves as an example of a military-style band, sporting dashing uniforms and several men wearing medals. The two boy cornet players seated cross-legged on either side of the drum draw the eye to the distinctive drummer at the centre of the group. The image was composed in about 1912 by Denton and Company, one of the town's earliest photographic businesses.

A somewhat bizarre assembly of men and boys outside the Miners Inn, Dodworth Bottom. The outrageous costumes and decorated building façade was in celebration of the coronation of George V on Thursday 22 June 1911, an occasion of great jubilation in the village and a welcome boost of trade for pub landlord Richard Dixon. Note the small comic band and the ambulance station notice below the inn sign. *Old Barnsley*

Boating and fishing were popular Edwardian pastimes and there was no better setting than Woolley Dam, a few miles to the north of Barnsley, which attracted huge crowds during the summer months and continued to do so until its drainage in 1951.

Churches and chapels often performed small costumed plays and musicals in order to raise funds, although *A Brahmin Wedding* was perhaps an unusual subject for Pitt Street Methodists. It was photographed by Lamb in about 1910.

But there was a large cast for *Zurika*, held in St Mary's church hall, Wombwell, in about 1928. Front row: (second from the left) Isobel Robinson, (third) Mary Fowler, (fifth) 'Robinson', (seventh) Miriam Wright. Second row: (first) Ethel Sharpe, (third) Joan Harrop, (sixth) Jack Shelton, (seventh) Ena Tingle, (eighth) Ian Tilbrook, (ninth) Beth Ibberson, (thirteenth) Jean Evans. Third row: (second) Turton, (sixth) Beryl Gleadhall, (seventh) Bessie Mellor. Back row: (fifth) John Tingle, (sixth) Stanley Barrowclough, (seventh) Sam Sharpe, (ninth) Beevers, (twelfth) Colin Harrop, (fourteenth) Eva Wilkinson.

The former Globe Picture House, photographed by the author in 1990 just before its demolition, was destroyed since part of the elegant building protruded into the planned route of the Western Relief Road. The Globe had been refurbished in 1981 and kept alive as a theatre, but sadly Barnsley Playgoers' *The Boyfriend* was its farewell attraction.

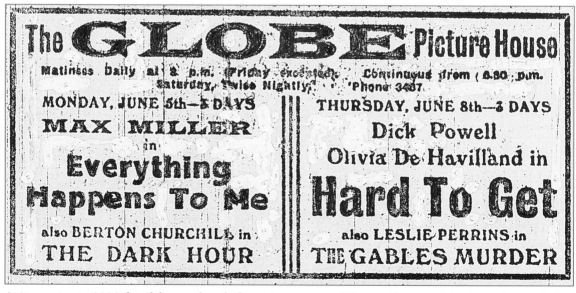

At its opening in 1914 the Globe was described as a 'new, cosy and thoroughly up to date picture house', in fact 'The Cinema Delux of the District'. This advert dates from 1939 when a Max Miller comedy and *Hard to Get*, starring Dick Powell and Olivia De Havilland, were the main feature films during a week when many young Barnsley men had to register for possible military service.

GLOBE CINEMA

BARNSLEY Tel.3467 *Cinema Car Park*

TONIGHT AND EVERY NIGHT AT 8 O'CLOCK

BINGO

One of our £50 Jackpots not won for 4 weeks was given away Monday, Tuesday, Wednesday. Also 20 really first class prizes in our new "Take your Pick" competition.

O'course it's the "Globe" New Street for

BINGO

Mrs. A. Sawyer, of Barnsley, won £270 on Wednesday.

AT YOUR

GLOBE CINEMA

FRIDAY TO MONDAY 10 p.m.

Thrills from the Continent

"ROULETTE CASINO"

MEMBERS ONLY

Coffee Bar open daily 6 p.m.

The great decline in cinema audiences during the 1950s and the rise of television ownershop resulted in the closure of many old cinemas. Some, like the Globe, were converted into bingo halls and even casinos, as can be seen by this advertisement, published in September 1962.

Pop group Dave Lincoln and the Senators, photographed by Ron Harris at Mansfield Road WMC, Athersley North, 1964. Left to right: Glyn Musgrave (lead guitar), singer Dave Lincoln (real name Pitt), Terry Osbourne (drums), Tony Hurd (bass guitar) and – with a 'Beatle' haircut, looking like John Lennon, John Hutchinson (rhythm guitar). Apart from clubs and pubs the group played at popular Barnsley area dance halls such as The Baths and Civic Hall, and backed top bands such as The Four Pennies, Wayne Fontana and the Mindbenders, Acker Bilk and Shane Fenton. *Harris Collection*

Marie and Peter Stott were 'mine hosts' at several Barnsley pubs including the Sportsman Inn, Smithies, when this photograph was taken in the early 1950s. There is no doubt that the man at the bar enjoying a well-earned pint was electricity worker Robert Featherstone, although a former Newhill Road neighbour is convinced that the photograph shows Bob at the opening of the Athersley Arms! *Harris Collection*

CELEBRATIONS & SPECIAL OCCASIONS

Hands in pockets, Bernard Harper (b. 1912), the twelfth of fourteen children (of the writer's great aunt), has his portrait taken on a day trip to Blackpool. Bernard worked at local pits until becoming a highly successful professional footballer, a half-back in more than 200 games for Barnsley during the 1930s, captaining the Reds' championship side of 1938/39. In December 1939 Harper replaced the great Stan Cullis in the England team, and had an 'outstanding' debut before joining the RAF.

This unusual group photograph was discovered at a postcard fair near Leeds and had the imprint 'Will Randall' embossed on its lower right corner – but the location and occasion are a mystery. An appeal through Kath Parkin's 'Memories' feature in the *Barnsley Chronicle* resulted in a positive identification by Don Walton who recognised his grandparents, uncles and cousins. It was a double-wedding celebration, seen outside the home of Frederick and Lucy Charlton, 24 Newton Street (off Summer Lane, Barnsley), whose daughters Florence and Lily had married Horace Young and James Charles Walton respectively at St John's Church on 1 June 1920. Front row, left to right: Lucy Charlton, Mrs Young (Horace's mother), Florence and Horace Young (bride and groom), Lily and James Walton (bride and groom), Sarah Walton (James's mother), Frederick Charlton, and Nellie 'Cissie' Charlton (a third daughter of Fred and Lucy). Standing behind her is Harold Walton, who was to marry Nellie a year later. Fifth from the left on the third row is William Charlton, brother of the two brides. Third from the right on the back row is Herbert Walton, a brother of the groom, James Charles.

This more conventional wedding photograph, by Lamb, was rescued from a house clearance. Fashion suggests a mid- to late 1920s date. Two individuals have been identified as Mrs Poynton Birkinshaw and her eldest daughter who later became Mrs Mary Webster (back row, first and second from the left). Both families have long-standing butchering businesses in Mapplewell and Staincross.

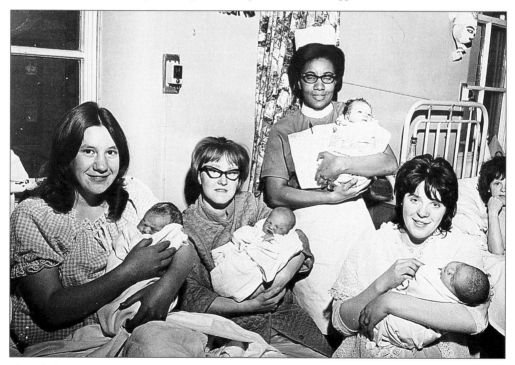

These babies were born at Barnsley District General Hospital on New Year's Day 1970, so will be celebrating their thirtieth birthdays at the millennium. The mum wearing glasses (centre) is Rita Wood, whose daughter Lisa Johnson was first to arrive at 12.30 am. The young mother on the left is Chris Chamberlaine with baby Nicola, while on the right is Irene Brodie and daughter Diane.

Darfield and District Conservative Club commissioned Warner Gothard to produce this splendid commemorative montage in honour of its First World War servicemen. It represents a new and important addition to the Gothard listing and may serve as a useful source for local and family historians.

Understandably glum-looking 'Belgium refugees' are featured in this quality photograph by Lamb, 1914. To achieve such a composition must have taken a great deal of mutual patience. Several men have clay pipes, two of the children hold teddy bears and a little girl shows off her doll. The only lady wearing a hat, seated in the centre, may have had some official role.

During the First World War St Edward's Vicarage was used as a servicemen's convalescence home. Matron Miss M.G. Bellamy is shown with a small group of patients. A commemorative tablet in the church records that 562 men received treatment, courtesy of E.G. Lancaster of Keresforth Hall, 'patron of this living'. One of a series of surviving photographs, this one by Lamb is precisely dated 15 March 1917.

The Yorkshire Agricultural Show came to Barnsley in August 1907 and was held on a field off Dodworth Road, across from the present Ford garage. The town had had some previous experience of the event, having hosted the show at short notice in 1880. Attendance was good – 46,386 over three days – but only producing a profit of £200. In the right foreground of this Gothard card the bandstand and seating are clearly visible, while trade and show buildings extend for a considerable distance. Just in view, with a backdrop of chimneys, is part of the main arena.

An 'orphan fund procession' passes through Cudworth village, a brass band and trade union banners to the fore, 1908. Children at street-level and onlookers at their doorways create a busy scene, and a commercial photographic subject.

King George V and Queen Mary in the town centre, 12 July 1912, just over a year since the coronation, three months after the sinking of the *Titanic* and Barnsley's FA Cup victory at Bramall Lane; and eight months before the creation of the new county borough. The royal itinerary included a memorable visit to Rylands Glassworks at Stairfoot, where workers sang to the Queen. The King is pictured (by Denton & Co.) in conversation with Alderman W.E. Raley and Mayor Joseph H. Cotterill.

There was a 'joyous atmosphere' in the town on Wednesday 27 October 1954 when the new Queen made her first visit. On arrival at the Exchange Station at about 10 a.m. Her Royal Highness and the Duke of Edinburgh were welcomed by the Lord Lieutenant of the West Riding (Earl of Scarbrough) and other dignitaries. Many local people took snapshots of the occasion, including this surviving example, which shows the Queen walking along Regent Street en route to the Town Hall, where gifts were presented by the Mayor and Mayoress (Alderman and Mrs A.E. McVie).

This royal 'walkabout' of 1975 is in startling contrast to the formalities of 1912. The Queen is clearly enjoying herself, joking with a packed crowd on Cheapside. In particular it was a great thrill for Mrs C. Banks and her sister Mrs M. Wilcock, to whom she spoke on this happy occasion.

'Queen of Hearts!' was the bold headline in the *Barnsley Chronicle* following the royal visit to the town on Friday 12 December 1986. Thousands of people braved the cold weather to catch a glimpse of the Queen as she travelled from Castlereagh Street to the town centre for lunch at the Town Hall. Mayor Jack Wood reported that she had enjoyed 'every minute' of her three-hour stay, absolutely delighted by the 'happy faces' of so many Barnsley people. This photograph was taken by the author as the Queen left the Town Hall.

CHAPTER EIGHT

DAILY TOIL

Samuel Marsland, with an almost military bearing, stands with his young team of bakers, holding a long-handled wooden 'peel' or shovel, used for inserting mixed dough into an oven. He ran a 'steam bakery' at 37 Shambles Street from 1896 to 1899. The oven, a rather grand affair, can be seen in the background. Marsland may have been one of the last of the old-style bakers who used gas and coal as power for mixing dough and heating ovens. A modern health inspector would approve of the appropriate headwear and aprons. Mr Marsland would have been well known to many people, since apart from the 'staff of life' his front shop sold a variety of confectionery items, and he operated a horse and cart delivery round.

Mobile traders sold their wares from horse-drawn wagons. Barrowclough was probably emblazoned on the side of this 'pots and pans' example, though the family's real name was Brown. Dating from about 1900, this rare photograph was probably taken in Hayes Croft, a typical Victorian courtyard. Standing on the wagon is licensed pedlar Tom Brown who was killed in the First World War. Maria, his wife, also known as 'Grandma Ria', carried on his trade and later rented heavy horses to bargees from her canalside caravan on Keel Field. To the left is Bob Nelson whose wife, Florrie, leans against the rear oak-hubbed wheel. Note the adjacent caravan, yard chickens and a few local residents, one peering at the staged event through an upper window.

Understandably most traders took great pride in both the condition and appearance of their horses; indeed there must have been rivalry caused by the polished brasses, leather and floral decoration. In charge are two other members of the 'Barrowcloughs', Oswald Brown and his brother Geoffrey. Oswald's 'peg-leg' was a consequence of a mining accident at Carlton.

Another mobile trader, Jonas Wildsmith, is captured by the lens of Will Randall in about 1907, the vendor's little dog perched on his two-wheeled cart adding interest to an otherwise dull composition. Jonas is listed in Kelly's 1928 directory as an 'iron, steel and machinery merchant' of Queen's Road, though his telegraph address ('Scrap, Wildsmith') is a more telling indication of his occupation – and clearly in keeping with the contents of his yard. Jonas commissioned this picture postcard to send before he visited local works.

This Edwardian photograph shows a blacksmith outside his workshop at Ardsley, a good site off the Barnsley–Doncaster road. With shirt sleeves rolled up and strong and skilful hands, he is standing at the side of a horse and surrounded by a variety of locals, especially children, all keen to pose for the camera. His 'shop' backs on to a dovecote. Ardsley had some of the most interesting buildings in the Barnsley area but few now survive. *Old Barnsley*

Hats were in fashion when this photograph by Lamb of a group of employees of the Barnsley Gas Company was taken outside the Old Mill gasometer, 1917. A meter can be seen at the foot of the works manager. Note the uniform and badges of the women meter readers, one of them identified as Helen Barton and another as Adelaide Asquith (second left, front row) while seated, fifth from the left in the middle row, is George Frudd, who conducted the 'Whit Sing' on Market Hill.

The Perseverance Estate (beween Dodworth Road and Summer Lane station) abattoir yard was, according the Barnsley British Co-operative history of 1903 'a well-arranged building . . . which tends to cleanliness' where carcasses were conveyed between buildings via a 'mechanical contrivance' and twenty-seven beasts could be 'dexterously' weighed in half an hour. Two workers demonstrate their skills in front of a pet dog and a live sheep!

Packers, sorters and case-makers at Wood Brothers' glassworks: this is one of a superb series of works photographs taken by Warner Gothard in 1908. The lad in the centre only looks about twelve years old. Note the suited foreman/manager who, as can be seen below, appears with another group of workers on the same day.

Another carefully arranged Gothard study of 'stoppers', 'cutters', 'bottle washers' and 'fitters' at the Pontefract Road works of Wood Brothers' Glass Company. This family business which began in Worsbrough Dale, moving to Hoyle Mill in about 1870, celebrated its centenary with similar photographs by the Denton Company in 1928. During the Second World War the company made aeroplane landing and navigation lights and chemistry measuring equipment, blown manually. Young lads carried molten glass to the annealing ovens. Many furnace men became 'unfit', moving to lighter jobs on the packing bay.

An informal 1950s photograph of workers at the Reynolds Brothers' car body repair shop, off Summer Lane. This family firm was one of the town's first automobile engineers, operating from its main works and garage on Peel Street. In 1908 it also boasted of being 'the largest cycle manufacturers' in the district. A 'deluxe Ford' could be purchased from Reynolds' for £135 in 1937 and a new Vauxhall Victor for £745 in 1962.

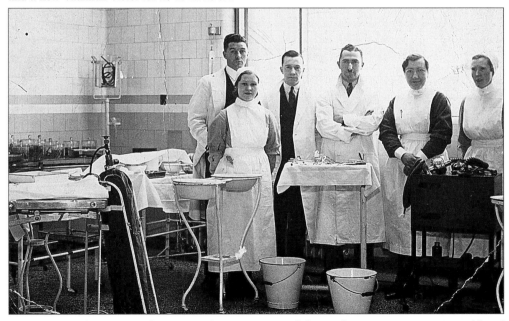

The operating theatre at Beckett Hospital, c. 1937. From left to right: Housemen Dr Fitzgerald and Dr Watson, House Surgeon Dr Isaac Rose, Theatre Sister Ryan and nurses Lindley and (on the left) England. This is the theatre where injured miners from the terrible Wharncliffe Woodmoor disaster of 1936 were treated, Dr Rose in particular doing much for burns and fractures. The hospital, founded by John Staniforth Beckett in 1864, closed in 1977 and was demolished two years later.

BRITAIN IN OLD PHOTOGRAPHS

SUTTON'S PHOTOGRAPHIC HISTORY OF TRANSPORT

To order any of these titles please telephone our distributor, Littlehampton Book Services on 01903 828800
For a catalogue of these and our other titles please ring Emma Leitch on 01453 731114